CARLOS ALCARAZ

BY LEIGH LEWIS

AMICUS LEARNING

**Inspire is published by
Amicus Learning, an imprint of Amicus**
P.O. Box 227
Mankato, MN 56002
www.amicuspublishing.us

Copyright © 2026 Amicus.
International copyright reserved in all countries.
No part of this book may be reproduced in any form
without written permission from the publisher.

Editor: Ana Brauer
Series Designer: Kathleen Petelinsek
Book Designer and Photo Researcher: Emily Dietz

Library of Congress Cataloging-in-Publication Data

Names: Lewis, Leigh, author.
Title: Carlos Alcaraz / by Leigh Lewis.
Description: Mankato, MN : Inspire is published by Amicus Learning, an imprint of Amicus, [2026] |
Series: Inspire | Includes bibliographical references and index. | Audience: Ages 5–9 years | Audience:
Grades 2–3 | Summary: "Learn about Spanish tennis star Carlos Alcaraz and his accomplishments in an
engaging profile packed with photos and fact-filled text suitable for young readers. Includes table of
contents, glossary, further resources, and index."— Provided by publisher.
Identifiers: LCCN 2024044107 (print) | LCCN 2024044108 (ebook) | ISBN 9798892005166 (lib. bdg.) |
ISBN 9798892005708 (paperback) | ISBN 9798892006248 (ebook)
Subjects: LCSH: Alcaraz, Carlos Garfia, 2003–Juvenile literature. | Tennis players—
Spain—Biography—Juvenile literature.
Classification: LCC GV994.A46 L49 2026 (print) | LCC GV994.A46 (ebook) |
DDC 796.342092 [B]—dc23/eng/20241211
LC record available at https://lccn.loc.gov/2024044107
LC ebook record available at https://lccn.loc.gov/2024044108

Photo Credits: Alamy Stock Photo/Collection Christophel, 12; Associated Press/
Abaca Press/Sipa USA, cover, Carlos Tischler/Eyepix Group, 18–19, Corinne Dubreuil/
Abaca Press, 14, 20; Getty Images/Clive Brunskill, 8, 9, 21, Diego Souto/Quality
Sport Images, 13, Mateo Villalba/Quality Sport Images, 10–11, Robert Szaniszlo/
NurPhoto, 17, Tim Clayton - Corbis, 4, Quality Sport Images, 7

Printed in India

Table of Contents

- 5 Tennis Star
- 6 Early Start
- 9 Tennis Family
- 10 Playing His Hero
- 12 Number One
- 15 Major Awards
- 16 All-Court Player
- 18 Helping Kids
- 20 The Olympics
- 22 Super Stats
- 23 Glossary
- 24 Read More
- 24 On the Web
- 24 Index

Carlos Alcaraz's nickname is Carlitos.

Tennis Star

Carlos Alcaraz steps up to the line. He throws the ball into the air. It's a perfect serve! The other player runs to return the ball. Alcaraz jumps and smashes it to the corner. He wins the match!

Carlos Alcaraz is a Spanish tennis star.

Early Start

In 2006, Alcaraz got his first tennis racquet. He was three years old. He started playing one year later. In 2018, he went **pro**. He was 15 years old. Alcaraz won many matches as a teen. In 2019, he won the Junior French Open. He was a junior champion!

Alcaraz quickly became a fan favorite in tennis.

Alcaraz's dad is one of his biggest supporters.

Tennis Family

Alcaraz comes from a tennis family. His dad was a pro player. He coached Alcaraz for a few years. Then he managed a tennis club. Alcaraz's grandfather started the tennis club.

DID YOU KNOW?
Alcaraz has three brothers. They all play tennis.

Alcaraz and Rafael Nadal talk before their match in 2022.

Playing His Hero

Picture your hero. Now think about playing against them. Alcaraz has always said that Spanish tennis player Rafael Nadal is his hero. He got the chance to play him in 2022. That was in the Madrid Open. Alcaraz won!

Number One

Alcaraz wanted to be the best. There were so many other good players. In 2021, he was **ranked** #32 in the world. With hard work, he improved. By the end of 2022, he became #1.

Alcaraz was ranked #1 after winning the 2022 US Open.

INSPIRATION
To prepare for a match, Alcaraz watches *Rocky IV* and listens to "Eye of the Tiger" by Survivor.

Alcaraz won his first Wimbledon Grand Slam trophy in 2023.

Major Awards

There are four **Grand Slam** tournaments. They are in the US, England, France, and Australia. Alcaraz has won three of them. He won the US Open in 2022, the French Open in 2024, and Wimbledon in 2023 and 2024.

RECORD HOLDER
As of 2024, Alcaraz is the youngest man to win the French Open and Wimbledon in the same year.

Alcaraz takes time to greet his fans before he plays.

Helping Kids

Alcaraz believes it is important to be a good tennis player AND a good person. He wants to help others. He started the Alcaraz **Foundation**. It helps children succeed in sports and in life. The foundation believes that all children should have the same opportunities.

The Olympics

In 2024, Alcaraz played in the Olympics. The games were in Paris. Alcaraz and Rafael Nadal represented Spain together in men's doubles. They lost in the quarterfinals. Alcaraz won a silver medal in men's singles! Fans look forward to what he will win next.

DREAM PAIRING
Alcaraz said it would be a dream to play doubles with Nadal in the Olympics. His dream came true!

Alcaraz waves at the crowd after winning a silver medal in the 2024 Olympics.

SUPER STATS

CARLOS ALCARAZ GARFIA

Nickname: Carlitos

Birthday: May 5, 2003

Hometown: El Palmar, Murcia, Spain

ACCOMPLISHMENTS

US Open Winner: 2022

Wimbledon Winner: 2023, 2024

French Open Winner: 2024

Olympics Silver Medalist: 2024

AWARDS

ATP (Association of Tennis Professionals) Newcomer of the Year: 2020

ATP Most Improved Player of the Year: 2022

Laureus World Sports Award for Breakthrough of the Year: 2023

GLOSSARY

baseline The line at the back of the court, farthest from the net. A player must serve from behind the baseline.

decoturf A hard court that has a little bit of cushion.

foundation An organization that gives money to help others.

Grand Slam The four most important tournaments in tennis: the French Open, the US Open, the Australian Open, and Wimbledon.

pro A professional sports player who is paid to play.

rank Based on tournament games played, a rank tells how good a player is compared to others.

READ MORE

Blue, Tyler. **Stars of World Tennis.** Abbeville Kids, 2024.

Dittmer, Lori. **Tennis.** Creative Education, 2020.

Laughlin, Kara L. **Tennis.** The Child's World, 2024.

ON THE WEB

Alcaraz Foundation
https://fundacionalcaraz.org/en/

Britannica Kids: Tennis
https://kids.britannica.com/kids/article/tennis/353847

INDEX

Alcaraz Foundation, 19
court, 16–17
family, 8–9
French Open, 15
Grand Slam, 14–15
Nadal, Rafael, 10–11, 20
Olympics, 20–21
ranking, 12
Rocky IV, 12
singles, 20
Wimbledon, 14, 15

About the Author

Leigh Lewis is a children's author who loves her three kids, traveling, pickleball, and telling stories. She has lived in the US, Russia, Japan, England, Greece, and Turkey. Check out her books at leighlewisbooks.com.